Spotter's Guide
ZOO
ANIMALS

Rosamund Kidman Cox

Consultant
Sue Mathews
of the Zoological Society of London

Illustrated by Malcolm McGregor
with additional illustrations by
Andy Martin

Contents

The author wishes to thank all the
zoos who kindly supplied her with
information about their collections.
In particular she wishes to thank the
Zoological Society of London and
Perth Zoological Gardens, Australia.

Series editor
Sue Jacquemier

First published in 1979 by
Usborne Publishing Limited,
20 Garrick Street, London WC2

Text and Artwork © 1979 by
Usborne Publishing Limited

Printed in Great Britain

How to use this book

This book is an identification guide to many of the animals that you will spot when you visit a zoo.

The book deals only with **mammals** (warm-blooded animals such as bears, that suckle their young), **birds** and **reptiles** (animals such as snakes). Fishes, insects and amphibians have been left out because not all zoos have collections of them.

Nocturnal animals (ones that are active mainly at night) are often kept together in the zoo, so we have put them in a section of their own in this book. There is also a section on **animals that are very rare in the wild** and therefore uncommon in zoos.

The **zoo guide** at the end of the book lists a number of zoos in Great Britain and Europe, North America, Australia and New Zealand. Look at this section to find out which is your nearest big zoo.

What the illustrations show
In the main colour section of the book each species or kind of animal

is grouped with animals that are related to it. For example, all the big cats (lions, tigers, etc.) are together.

The description next to each animal tells you the general area where the animal comes from, if it is rare in the wild, and a little about its behaviour. At the end of the description, its height or length is given (see below).

Sometimes both the male (♂) and the female (♀) are shown for one species. If the sexes look alike, there is no symbol.

When you spot an animal in a zoo, tick it off in the small circle next to its description.

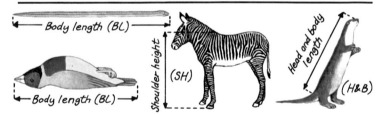

Measurements
Different kinds of animals are measured in different ways to give the most useful information. For birds and reptiles in this book the total body lengths (BL), including the tail, are given. Most mammals' measurements are of head and body

length (H&B) only (not including the tail), but for hoofed animals the shoulder height (SH) is given. The measurements are usually averages, but some are the maximum size of the animal, and this often means that one sex is very much larger than the other.

Visiting a zoo or safari park

The best time to go
Animals are usually most active in early morning and late afternoon.

The zoo map
Buy a map when you arrive and find out where the various groups of animals are. Decide which are your favourite animals and visit them first. If you have lots of time you could mark out your own route on the map and make a time-table. On the map below there is an example of a route.

Feeding times
The main notice board will tell you when these are. Do not be tempted to feed the animals. Their keepers give them suitable diets. Extra food will make them fat and may make them sick. **Tell a keeper** if you see

anyone giving an animal harmful objects like plastic bags or coins, or if you see someone teasing an animal.

New arrivals and baby animals
Look on the main notice board for information. Zoos breed as many animals as possible so that they do not have to take new animals from the wild. **Tell a keeper** if you see animals mating or being born; sometimes special arrangements have to be made for births.

Safari parks and zoo parks
In parks, animals are kept in large enclosures, so you may have to travel round by car, or in the park train. Try to borrow binoculars before you go so that you can look closely at any nervous animals.

1 Main notice board 10·05
2 Crocodile house 10·15
3 New Polar Bear Cub 10·45
4 Big cats' feeding time 11·00
5 Café 11·30
6 Reptile house 12·00
7 Giant Tortoise 12·30
Depart 1·00

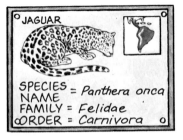

Latin names

When you look at the label on an animal's house, you will see a Latin **species name** as well as the English name. In different zoos, the English name may change, but the Latin name will always be the same. There will also be a Latin **family name** and an **order name**.

You can tell if two animals are closely related (for example, the Jaguar and the Tiger) if part of their Latin species name is the same. If just their family or order names are the same, they are also related, though not so closely.

LION
Carnivore

ZEBRA
Herbivore

BEAR
Omnivore

Tusks used for fighting

HIPPOPOTAMUS
Herbivore

Feeding

If you see an animal yawning, look at its teeth. They may be a clue to the kind of food it eats.

Meat-eaters are called **carnivores.** Long pointed **canine teeth** at each side of the upper and lower jaws help them tear meat. Birds of prey have sharp beaks and claws.

Vegetarian animals (plant-eaters) are called **herbivores**; their teeth get worn down by chewing plants. Some herbivores have teeth which grow continuously to make up for this. Feeding on plants on the ground is called **grazing** and feeding on trees and bushes is called **browsing**.

Animals which eat both plants and meat are called **omnivores.** Some insect-eating mammals have no teeth; they have long, mobile tongues or hard gums.

In the food trays of most animals in the zoo you will see a mixture of natural and artificial foods (like pellets); artificial foods provide a balanced diet, as it is impossible to give the animal everything it would eat in the wild.

Making a notebook

Making a record sheet
Zoos are good places in which to study animal behaviour. If you make several visits to the same zoo, you could choose a favourite animal and make a study of it.

Write on the record sheet as many details as you can about the animal. Clip the sheet to a board so that you can make notes when you are at the zoo.

Drawings and notes
Make drawings or diagrams to show how the animal walks, the position in which it sleeps, what its feet and teeth look like. Record whether it is adult or young. Make notes on your drawings to show colouring – male, female and young may be different colours. Different - sized animals may be different sexes or ages; if the sexes are alike you may be able to tell them apart by their behaviour.

Note down any behaviour you see or special details about the animal. For example, some animals have a **prehensile tail.** This holds onto branches like a fifth limb. Note down what food is in the cage.

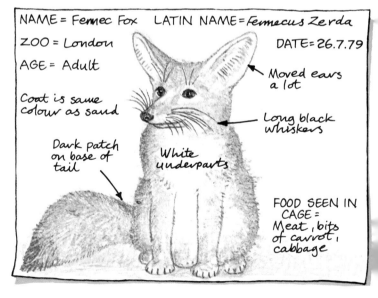

NAME = Fennec Fox   LATIN NAME = Fennecus Zerda
ZOO = London   DATE = 26.7.79
AGE = Adult
Coat is same colour as sand
Moved ears a lot
Long black whiskers
Dark patch on base of tail
White underparts
FOOD SEEN IN CAGE = Meat, bits of carrot, cabbage

Watching groups of zoo animals

If the animal you are studying lives in a group, make notes on the group behaviour. The record sheet below shows the sort of notes you could make. So that you can remember which animal is which, give each individual a number or name and make a short description of it.

There may be a **dominant** animal: it is the most bossy one. Make notes on how members of the group **communicate**. For example, they may make noises, or face and body movements. If you visit the zoo several times you will begin to learn what the animals' behaviour means.

A record sheet for a group of animals

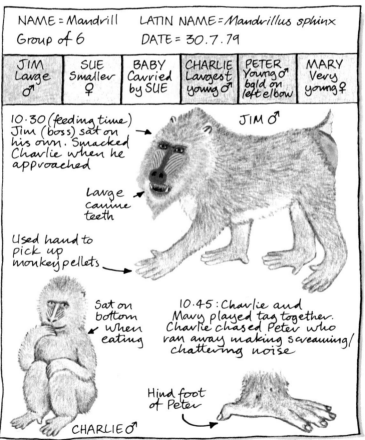

NAME = Mandrill   LATIN NAME = Mandrillus sphinx
Group of 6   DATE = 30.7.79

| JIM Large ♂ | SUE Smaller ♀ | BABY Carried by SUE | CHARLIE Largest young ♂ | PETER Young ♂ bald on left elbow | MARY Very young ♀ |

10.30 (feeding time) Jim (boss) sat on his own. Smacked Charlie when he approached

JIM ♂

Large canine teeth

Used hand to pick up monkey pellets

Sat on bottom when eating

10.45: Charlie and Mary played tag together. Charlie chased Peter who ran away making screaming/chattering noise

Hind foot of Peter

CHARLIE ♂

Apes

This is the name of the group of animals that the species on this page belong to.

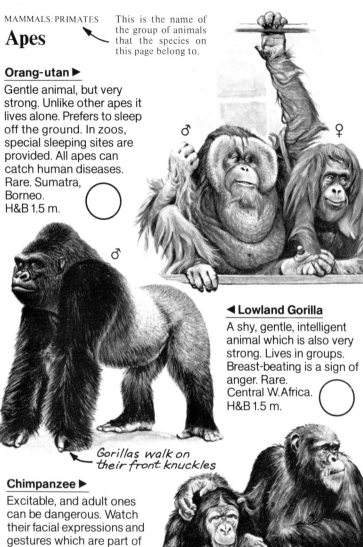

Orang-utan ▶

Gentle animal, but very strong. Unlike other apes it lives alone. Prefers to sleep off the ground. In zoos, special sleeping sites are provided. All apes can catch human diseases. Rare. Sumatra, Borneo.
H&B 1.5 m.

◀ Lowland Gorilla

A shy, gentle, intelligent animal which is also very strong. Lives in groups. Breast-beating is a sign of anger. Rare.
Central W.Africa.
H&B 1.5 m.

Gorillas walk on their front knuckles

Chimpanzee ▶

Excitable, and adult ones can be dangerous. Watch their facial expressions and gestures which are part of their language. Pink swellings on the female's bottom show she is ready to mate. Rare.
Central W.Africa.
H&B 1 m.

Gibbon, Monkeys

Lar/White-handed Gibbon ▶

Lives in pairs with young.
Notice how it moves by
swinging rather than
climbing. Listen for its
loud, hooting call.
Rare. S.E. Asia.
H&B 50 cm.

The Gibbon can swing along very fast using its long arms

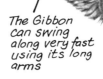

↖ *No tail*

Pig-tailed Macaque ▶

Lives in large groups. The
pouting face of a dominant
male is a greeting or a
threat. Try to spot the
leader male.
S.E. Asia.
Max. H&B 60 cm.

Flesh coloured rump

♂

♂

◀ Gelada Baboon

Female's red chest patch is
brightest at mating time.
Angry male flashes his
white eyelids and flips his
lips back to expose gums
and canine teeth.
Ethiopia. Max.
H&B 70 cm.

◀ Mandrill

Leader male is largest and
has the most brightly
coloured face and rump.
He sometimes makes a
barking noise. Look for his
long canine teeth.
W. Africa.
H&B 80 cm.

♂

9

Monkeys

Vervet Monkey ▶

Lives in large groups. In zoos, monkeys of the same sex fight unless they are parents and young. Grooming is a way of being friendly.
Africa.
H&B 60 cm.

Patas Monkey ▶

You will see it on the ground, but it sleeps in branches. Females are very possessive of their young.
C. and S. Africa.
H&B 80 cm.

♂

◀ Abyssinian Colobus

Shy, spending most of the time in branches. Babies may be passed around between the females. Has a croaking call.
Vegetarian. Africa.
H&B 65 cm.

◀ Proboscis Monkey

The nose grows throughout life; the male's is longer than the female's. They make snorting noises. When alarmed, the male makes a honking call and his nose straightens.
Rare. Borneo.
H&B 75 cm.

♂

South American Monkeys

Squirrel Monkey ▶

Lives in big groups. Runs along branches on all fours, using its tail as a balance.
S. America.
H&B 35 cm.

Prehensile tail

Humboldt's Woolly Monkey ▶

Has a prehensile tail which can grip branches like a fifth limb, or even pick up bits of food.
S. America.
H&B 70 cm.

♂

The male often carries the young

◀ White-faced Saki

Easily frightened and makes loud, bird-like alarm calls. The male helps carry the young. S. America.
Max. H&B 50 cm.

◀ Common Marmoset

Can only be kept in pairs. Male often carries young, giving them to female for feeding. Bird-like calls. S. America.
H&B 20 cm.

Lemurs, Tree Shrew, Sloth

Ruffed Lemur ▶

Colouring may also be a mixture of red, black and white. Makes loud, barking calls when angry or upset. Makes huge leaps between branches using its long hind legs. Rare. Madagascar. H&B 60 cm.

Ring-tailed Lemur ▶

May live in big groups. Females are dominant to males. Males have a special scratching claw on the wrist. Both sexes mark territory by rubbing chest and genital scent glands on branches. Madagascar. H&B 40 cm.

Two claws on front feet

◀ Common Tree-shrew

Very fast mover. Young are left in a separate nest, tended by mother every two days or so. S.E. Asia. H&B 20 cm.

◀ Two-toed Sloth

Sleeps, eats, mates and gives birth upside-down. Slow mover and almost helpless on the ground. Eats mainly leaves and digests food slowly. S. America. H&B 60 cm.

Elephants, Anteater

Indian Elephant

To keep its skin in good condition, it needs frequent baths. In the zoo, it eats up to 100 kg of food a day. All elephants are herbivores. Rare. S.E.Asia. Max. SH 3 m.

African Elephant

The largest land mammal. Most elephants in zoos are females as males can be uncontrollable. Births in zoos are therefore uncommon. Rare. Africa. Max. SH 4 m.

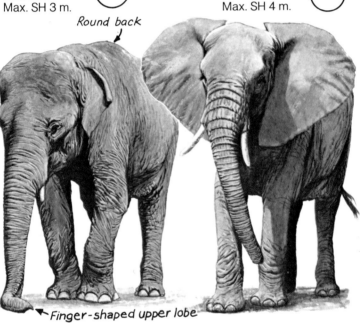

Round back

Finger-shaped upper lobe

Giant Anteater ▶

Sleeps for most of the day, its tail curled round it. Has no teeth; in wild, eats ants with its long sticky tongue. Zoo diet is mainly eggs and meat. C.and S.America. H&B 1 m.

Long, curved claws on feet

13

Dolphin, Seals

Bottlenosed Dolphin ▶

Difficult to keep in zoos.
Easily bored and may
develop unnatural
behaviour as a result.
Communicates with
whistles and squeaks. Has
a sonar system which can
locate an object at a
distance without
touching it.
World-wide.
Max. H&B 3.6 m.

It breathes out through its blowhole

Ear flaps

Sealions turn their hind feet forward when walking

◀ Californian Sealion

Lives in the sea in wild,
but does not mind fresh
water in zoos. Swims by
moving fore-limbs. When
coat is dry it is light fawn.
Males called bulls, females
called cows.
N.Pacific coasts.
Max. H&B 2.3 m.

Grey Seal ▶

Not a good acrobat like
the Sealion. Finds
movement on land difficult.
Try to time how long it
stays under water (up to
15 minutes). It closes its
nostrils under water and
swims with its hind limbs.
Babies have white fur.
N.Atlantic coasts.
Max. H&B 3.1 m.

The seal's hind feet are useless on land

No external ear

Zebras, Horse, Tapir

Grant's Zebra ▶

Spot the species by their rump patterns. **Grevy's**, the largest, has a cry like a donkey. Rare. The **Common Zebra** species includes **Grant's** and **Chapman's** zebras. Both have a barking call. The **Mountain Zebra** is the smallest species; it neighs like a horse. Rare. Africa. Max. SH 1.1 m.

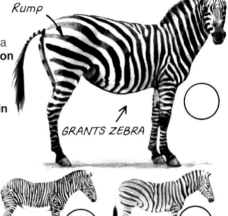

Rump

GRANTS ZEBRA

MOUNTAIN ZEBRA   GREVY'S ZEBRA   CHAPMAN'S ZEBRA

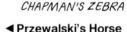

Stiff mane

White muzzle

◀ Przewalski's Horse

Pronounced "pris-vaal-ski". The only living wild horse, saved from extinction by breeding in zoos. A stud-book listing the horses and their ancestors helps zoos swap animals to prevent inbreeding. Mongolia. SH 1.1 m.

◀ Malayan Tapir

Herbivore. Uses its long lips to pluck food. Feet are designed for swampy ground and get sore on very hard ground. S.E.Asia. Other Tapirs come from S.America. Rare. SH 1.1 m.

15

Rhinoceros, Hippopotamus

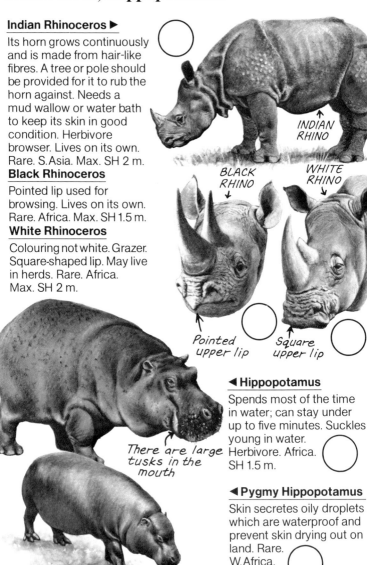

Indian Rhinoceros ▶

Its horn grows continuously and is made from hair-like fibres. A tree or pole should be provided for it to rub the horn against. Needs a mud wallow or water bath to keep its skin in good condition. Herbivore browser. Lives on its own. Rare. S. Asia. Max. SH 2 m.

Black Rhinoceros

Pointed lip used for browsing. Lives on its own. Rare. Africa. Max. SH 1.5 m.

White Rhinoceros

Colouring not white. Grazer. Square-shaped lip. May live in herds. Rare. Africa. Max. SH 2 m.

INDIAN RHINO

BLACK RHINO

WHITE RHINO

Pointed upper lip

Square upper lip

There are large tusks in the mouth

◀ Hippopotamus

Spends most of the time in water; can stay under up to five minutes. Suckles young in water. Herbivore. Africa. SH 1.5 m.

◀ Pygmy Hippopotamus

Skin secretes oily droplets which are waterproof and prevent skin drying out on land. Rare. W. Africa. SH 1 m.

Peccary, Camel, Llama

Collared Peccary ▶

This is not a true pig. If excited, hair over a scent gland near the tail base sticks up and you will smell a musky scent. Young are reddish with a black back-stripe.
C.and S.America.
SH 50 cm.

The Peccary has a scent gland here

Winter coat

Protective skin on the "knees"

◀ Bactrian Camel

A two-humped camel from Asia. The **Dromedary** from Arabia has one hump. Both are used for riding and carrying loads. Humps do not store water but contain fat deposits, used if there is no food. Feet have broad soles to help them walk on sand in the wild. Look moth-eaten in spring when they moult.
SH 1.8 m.

Llama ▶

Related to camels and, like them, may spit when angry. Can be many colours. Related to the **Guanaco** which is more slender with a red-brown coat. Lives in groups with one leader male.
S.America.
SH 1.2 m.

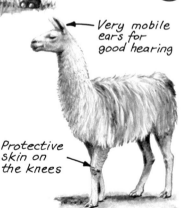

Very mobile ears for good hearing

Protective skin on the knees

Giraffe, Okapi

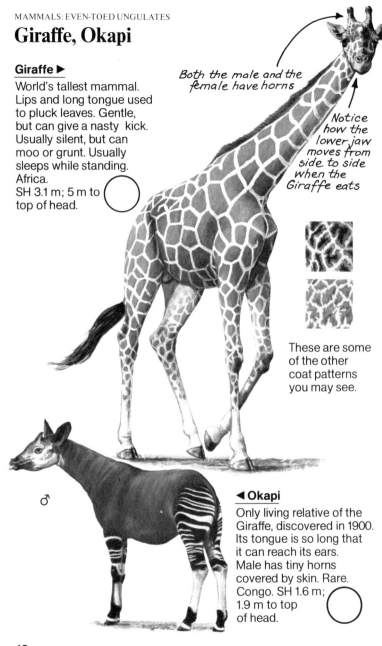

Giraffe ▶
World's tallest mammal.
Lips and long tongue used
to pluck leaves. Gentle,
but can give a nasty kick.
Usually silent, but can
moo or grunt. Usually
sleeps while standing.
Africa.
SH 3.1 m; 5 m to
top of head.

*Both the male and the
female have horns*

*Notice
how the
lower jaw
moves from
side to side
when the
Giraffe eats*

These are some
of the other
coat patterns
you may see.

♂

◀ Okapi
Only living relative of the
Giraffe, discovered in 1900.
Its tongue is so long that
it can reach its ears.
Male has tiny horns
covered by skin. Rare.
Congo. SH 1.6 m;
1.9 m to top
of head.

18

Deer

Père David's Deer ▶

Extinct in the wild and today can only be seen in zoos; breeding is therefore very important. Has a dark winter coat and a light summer coat. Lives in large herds with a leader stag. He will fight with rivals. Originally from China.
SH 1.1 m.

The skin has been rubbed off these antlers

Summer coat

♂

These antlers have velvety skin on them

Both sexes have antlers

♂

◀ Reindeer

Like all deer, sheds its antlers each year; new ones are covered with skin which is eventually rubbed off. Eats lichen in wild and in some zoos.
Arctic.
SH 1.3 m.

Broad hooves for walking on snow

Reeves' Muntjac ▶

Male has small antlers. Alarm call is a bit like a dog's bark. Notice that when it runs, its head is held low. China. Escaped animals are wild in S.England.
SH 50 cm.

♂

Antelopes

Common Oryx/Gemsbok ▶

Like all antelopes, it never sheds its horns. It may use them for fighting. Africa. SH 1.2 m.

Scimitar-horned Oryx

Like all Oryx, it is quite rare in the wild, therefore breeding in zoos is important. Sahara. SH 1 m.

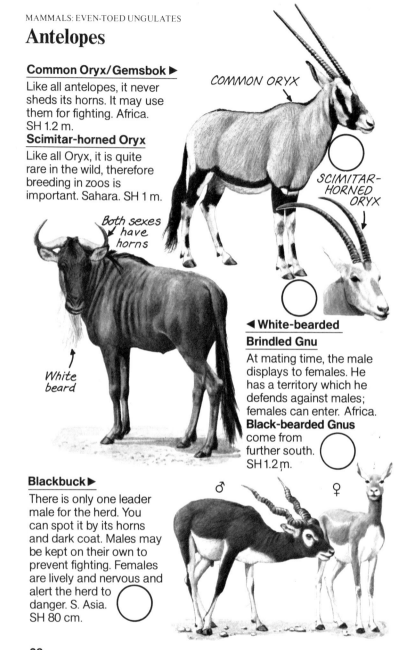

COMMON ORYX

SCIMITAR-HORNED ORYX

Both sexes have horns

White beard

◀ White-bearded
Brindled Gnu

At mating time, the male displays to females. He has a territory which he defends against males; females can enter. Africa.

Black-bearded Gnus

come from further south. SH 1.2 m.

Blackbuck ▶

There is only one leader male for the herd. You can spot it by its horns and dark coat. Males may be kept on their own to prevent fighting. Females are lively and nervous and alert the herd to danger. S. Asia. SH 80 cm.

♂   ♀

Antelopes, Bison

Blue Duiker ▶

This species includes
Maxwell's Duiker, also
found in zoos. Small, shy
antelope. Rubs sub-orbital
glands against objects to
mark out its
territory.
Africa. SH 40 cm.

Both sexes have horns

Suborbital gland

Small hump

♂

◀ Greater Kudu

The female is smaller than
the male and does not
have horns or a fringe on
her throat. In zoos, Kudus
are kept in groups with
only one male.
Mainly a browser.
Africa.
Max. SH 1.6 m.

American Bison ▶

Bellows when angry.
Heavy, but can move fast.
Likes rolling in mud and
dust. May look shaggy in
spring when moulting.
There is also a **European
Bison.** Rare.
N. America.
SH 2.6 m.

Ox, Saiga, Sheep, Goat

Musk Ox ▶

Under the coarse hair is a fine, woolly undercoat. In the wild. a herd will stand in line or in a circle to face an attacker.
Rare. Arctic.
SH 1.3 m.

Large wide feet

Saiga ▶

Only the male has horns. Nose is lined with mucus and hair, and in the wild this may warm inhaled air. The male can inflate his nose. The winter coat is white and shaggy. S.Russia.
SH 70 cm.

Summer coat

♂

Both sexes have horns

♂

Fringe

Summer coat

♂

Beard

◀ Barbary Sheep

Not closely related to domestic sheep. The only wild sheep with a throat-fringe. Both sexes have horns.
N.Africa.
SH 1 m.

◀ Markhor

Lives in herds usually led by an old female. Unlike sheep, all goats have beards. This is the largest wild goat. Rare. Himalayas.
SH 1 m.

22

Australian pouched animals

Long-nosed Potoroo ▶

Related to the Kangaroo, but when hopping does not keep its body upright. Builds nests, carrying nest material with its tail. Nocturnal in the wild. Australia. H&B 40 cm.

The female is usually grey

RED ♂ KANGAROO

GREY KANGAROO

◀ Western Grey Kangaroo

Has powerful back legs and can jump a 2 m fence. Like most marsupials, the young are tiny and naked when born. They climb up to the pouch and develop inside it. They first poke their heads out when they are 200 days old and leave the pouch when they are 300 days old.

Red Kangaroo

Has white face marks and a pale tail tip. Female may be grey. Australia. H&B 1.5 m.

When sitting it uses its tail as a prop

Common Wombat ▶

Loves digging. Partly nocturnal and will spend most of the day in its burrow. The pouch opens backwards which may stop earth going in as it moves forward. Australia. H&B 1.2 m.

Its teeth grow continuously

Gnawing animals

Canadian Beaver ▶

The family lives in a "lodge" made of sticks and mud, with an underwater entrance. The main chamber is above water. The Beaver is most active in the late afternoon and at night.
N.America.
H&B 1 m.

The Beaver slaps the water with its tail as an alarm signal ↓

Mara ▶

Related to the Guineapig. When moving at speed, may hop like a rabbit. In the wild, lives in big groups which dig large burrow systems.
S.America.
H&B 70 cm.

Unlike most rodents, the Mara walks on its toes ↓

◀ Siberian Chipmunk

Ground-living squirrel. Very active. Carries food in its large cheek pouches and may store food in its nest-box.
N.Europe and
Asia. H&B 10 cm.

◀ Black-tailed Prairie Dog

Ground-living squirrel, Alarm cry is a bark. Lives in large groups which dig burrows. The group of burrows is called a "town".
N.America.
H&B 30 cm.

The Prairie Dog's long claws are used for digging →

Wolf, Jackal, Hunting Dog, Fox

Grey Wolf ▶

The pack has a territory whose boundaries are scent-marked with urine. Group howling helps attachments form between all the pack members, and in the wild warns other packs of their presence. Europe, N. America, Asia. Max. H&B 1.2 m.

Black-backed Jackal ▶

Lives in pairs and is active mainly at night. Shy. Related to wolves and dogs. S. and E. Africa. Other jackals are found in Asia. Max. H&B 90 cm.

◀ African Hunting Dog

Listen for its strange hooting call. Like the wolf, lives in a group which has a strict social order. Coat markings vary in colour and pattern. Africa. Max. H&B 1.1 m.

It has very strong jaws

◀ Arctic Fox

One form is dark bluish-grey in summer and pale bluish-grey in winter. Another form is brown in summer and white in winter. Arctic regions. Max. H&B 78 cm.

Winter coat

Summer coat

Hyena, Otter, Coati, Meerkat

Spotted/Laughing
Hyaena ▶

Makes its "laughing"/
chattering cry at mating
time. Often howls. In the
wild, nocturnal; lives in
groups and feeds on dead
animals.
Africa.
H&B 85 cm.

It has strong jaws used for crunching bones

When climbing it uses its tail as a balance

Ring-tailed Coati ▶

In the wild, females live in
groups; in zoos, male is
removed when there are
young. C. and S.
America.
Max. H&B 65 cm.

It is always sniffing things with its long nose

◀ Suricate Meerkat

Related to mongooses.
Often sits upright in front
of its hole, watching for
danger. In the wild, lives in
big groups in
burrows. S. Africa.
H&B 30 cm.

◀ Canadian Otter

Partly nocturnal. Can only
be kept in pairs. Loves
water acrobatics, but also
spends much time on land.
Male is aggressive at
mating time.
N. America.
H&B 1 m.

When swimming, it uses its tail as a rudder

Webbed feet ➜

Bears

Asiatic Black Bear ▶

Dangerous, like all bears, and can kill with one swipe of its paw. In cold weather, may stay in its den. The **American Black Bear** does not usually have a white V on its chest. Omnivore.
C. and E. Asia.
Max. H&B 1.6 m.

Standing on two legs is a threat sign

Long claws

◀ Brown Bear

Like all bears, walks on all fours, but can sit and stand and often lies on its back sunbathing. A good climber. The brown fur of the **American Grizzly** is tipped with white and grey. Europe, Asia.
Max. H&B 2.8 m.

Polar Bear ▶

Needs a large pool to swim in. In zoos, pregnant females must be kept in their dens to give birth and not disturbed until the cubs are about three months old. Rare. Arctic regions.
H&B 2.5 m.

The soles of its feet are hairy

27

Bear, Pandas

Malayan Sun Bear ▶
A tropical bear which needs a lot of warmth. In the wild, builds tree nests for sleeping in. Like other bears, is a good climber. Omnivore.
S.E. Asia.
Max. H&B 1.4 m.

U-shaped chest marking

Naked soles

◀ Giant Panda
Not a true bear. Prefers to live on its own. Has special pads on its hands to help it hold bamboo. Its diet includes many kilos of bamboo a day. You may see it rubbing its bottom on the ground; this is to scent-mark its territory. Likes to climb.
Rare. China.
H&B 1.5 m.

Bamboo

Red Panda ▶
Like its closest relative, the Giant Panda, it sleeps in the middle of the day. Its nest-box is placed high off the ground as it is a good climber.
Himalayas.
Max. H&B 65 cm.

Cats

Serval ▶
Runs fast over short distances, but does not climb very much. Listen for its repetitive, yowling cry. It has acute hearing. Africa. H&B 95 cm.

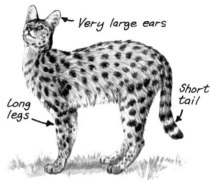

Very large ears

Long legs

Short tail

Wild Cat ▶
Looks like a domestic cat, but is larger and stronger. Has a broad head and bushy, ringed tail. Mostly nocturnal in the wild. Europe, W. Asia, Africa. H&B 60 cm.

Bushy tail

◀ Ocelot
Like all cats, it sprays certain places with urine; this marks its territory and helps the male know if the female is ready to mate. Rare. C. and S. America. Max. H&B 1.3 m.

◀ Jungle Cat
Spends most time on the ground, but can climb. Like all cats, it can pull back its claws into a skin sheath. This stops them getting blunt. S. Asia. H&B 60 cm.

Cats

Puma/Cougar ▶

Usually silent, but it yowls and screams at mating time; it also purrs. The kittens have spots on their backs and sides.
N. and S. America.
Max. H&B 2 m.

Northern Lynx ▶

Hisses when angry and two tufts of fur on its throat stick out. In the wild, it grows a thick winter coat.
N. America, N. Asia, N. Europe.
Max. H&B 1.3 m.

Ear tufts — Winter coat

Large feet help it walk on snow

Ear tufts

Short tail

◀ Caracal

Most cats signal with their tail and white spots on the backs of their ears. The Caracal's ear tufts replace spots, but their true function is not known.
Africa, W. Asia.
H&B 70 cm.

◀ Clouded Leopard

Smaller than the ordinary Leopard. Uses its long, heavy tail as a balance when climbing. Very long canine teeth.
Rare. S. E. Asia.
H&B 95 cm.

Very long tail

Short legs

Cats

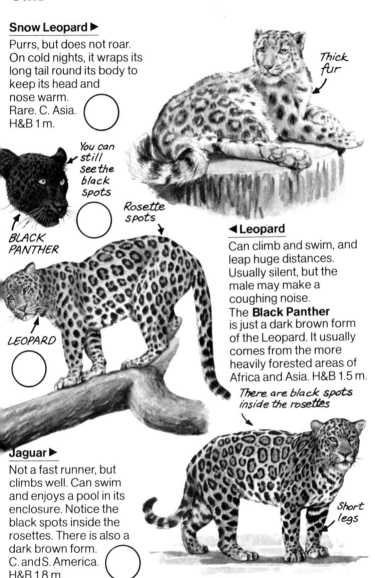

Snow Leopard ▶
Purrs, but does not roar.
On cold nights, it wraps its
long tail round its body to
keep its head and
nose warm.
Rare. C. Asia.
H&B 1 m.

Thick fur

You can still see the black spots

BLACK PANTHER

Rosette spots

◀ Leopard
Can climb and swim, and
leap huge distances.
Usually silent, but the
male may make a
coughing noise.
The Black Panther
is just a dark brown form
of the Leopard. It usually
comes from the more
heavily forested areas of
Africa and Asia. H&B 1.5 m.

LEOPARD

There are black spots inside the rosettes

Jaguar ▶
Not a fast runner, but
climbs well. Can swim
and enjoys a pool in its
enclosure. Notice the
black spots inside the
rosettes. There is also a
dark brown form.
C. and S. America.
H&B 1.8 m.

Short legs

Cats

Lion ▶

Unlike most cats, lives in big groups. Inactive much of the time. In the wild, females do most of the hunting. At mating time, female sprays objects with urine. Africa, S. W. Asia. Max. H&B 2.5 m.

The female has no mane

♂

WHITE TIGER

◀ Tiger

The largest of the cats. Lives on its own. Loves swimming, but seldom climbs. There are several races, varying in size and coat length and colour. The **White Tiger** is a pale form of the Indian Tiger. Rare. Asia. Max. H&B 3 m.

Cheetah ▶

Runs very fast over short distances. Young ones have a silver mane down their backs. Rare. Africa. Max. H&B 2 m.

Long legs

It can only partially retract its claws

Flightless birds

Emu ▶

Notice how its feathers look hairy. Like the Cassowary, the male Emu keeps the eggs warm and rears young without help from the female. Listen for its booming call.
Australia.
BL 2 m.

Three toes

♂

♀

Unlike other birds, it only has two toes

◀ Ostrich

Largest bird in the world. Runs very fast on its powerful, long legs. Can give a nasty forward kick. A male lives with several females who lay their eggs in the same nest; eggs are kept warm mainly by the male.
Africa. BL 2.4 m.

Casque

Australian Cassowary ▶

One of its three toes has a long dagger-like claw which it uses for attack or defence. It usually lives alone. Will hiss to make intruders go away. Australia.
BL 1.5 m.

This toe is used for fighting

Three toes

33

Flamingos, Goose

Greater Flamingo ▶

All flamingos live in large groups. In the wild their natural food contains a chemical which makes their feathers pink. In zoos this chemical may be added to their food. They feed by holding their heads upside-down and sifting water through the bill. Food is trapped by special filters. W.Asia. BL 1.4 m.

Lesser Flamingo

Smallest species. Africa, S.Asia. BL 85 cm.

Chilean Flamingo

This is a "race" or form of the Greater Flamingo. S. America. BL 1 m.

Caribbean/Rosy Flamingo

Another race of the Greater Flamingo. Galapagos Islands, Caribbean coasts. BL 1.2 m.

GREATER FLAMINGO

LESSER FLAMINGO

Lots of black on the bill

CARIBBEAN FLAMINGO

Red Knee-caps

CHILEAN FLAMINGO

◀ Hawaiian Goose/Né Né

Nearly became extinct, but zoo-bred birds are now being released into the wild. Males can be very aggressive. Hawaii. Max. BL 73 cm.

Penguins, Duck, Ibis

King Penguin

Has to be fed by hand, each fish being placed into its mouth. Male and female take turns to incubate the single egg. Penguins cannot fly, but spend a lot of time swimming (on or under the water). Watch how they propel themselves with their wings. It is rather like flying in water. Antarctic. BL 94 cm.

Black-footed Jackass Penguin

Makes a braying, croaking noise. Sub-Arctic. BL 72 cm.

Rockhopper Penguin

Antarctic and Sub-Arctic. BL 56 cm.

KING PENGUIN

BLACK-FOOTED JACKASS PENGUIN

ROCKHOPPER PENGUIN

"Sail" feathers. These are lost in summer

♂

Bill turns black in the breeding season

◄ Mandarin Duck

The male uses his bright colours and "sail" feathers to court the dull-brown female. They perch and nest in trees. China. BL 43 cm.

◄ Scarlet Ibis

Like many water birds in zoos, often "washes" bits of food in its drinking water before eating. S. America. BL 58 cm.

35

Crane, Stork, Pelican

Crowned Crane ▶

In spring, watch out for their courtship dance. Both sexes flap their wings, leap into the air and make loud cries. May pair for life. Eat mainly small mammals (eg. mice). E.Africa. BL 1.1 m.

◀ Marabou Stork

One of the largest storks. Usually silent, but like most storks, rattles its bill loudly when courting. In the wild it eats carrion (dead meat). Africa. BL 1.3 cm.

The function of the neck pouch is unknown

Skin pouch

European White Pelican ▶

Lives in large groups. Uses its pouched beak as a scoop for catching fish in the wild. Waddles like a duck, but can swim and fly well. E.Europe, Asia, S.Africa. BL 1.5 m.

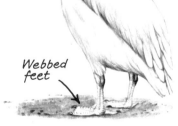

Webbed feet

Pheasants, Guineafowl

Indian Peafowl ▶

Only the male (peacock) has long feathers. He fans them out and vibrates them when courting a female (peahen). Listen for his loud shrieking call. India. BL 2 m.

♀ ♂

Golden Pheasant ▶

The male displays to the brown female by standing side on to her with his ruff feathers and wings spread to reveal the golden colour. Perches off the ground like all pheasants. W.China. BL 1 m.

♂

All pheasants and peafowl lose their long "covert" feathers after the mating season

♂

◀ Lady Amherst Pheasant

As with all pheasants and peafowl, what looks like the tail is really a collection of long "covert" feathers. The true tail is hidden under them. China. BL 1.5 m.

◀ Helmeted Guineafowl

Listen for its noisy metallic cry. Perches off the ground. Africa. BL 55 cm.

Owls, Caracara

Snowy Owl ▶

Like most owls, mainly nocturnal, but in zoos often awake in the day. In the wild, its colouring camouflages it against snow. Young ones have pale brown fluffy feathers. Arctic regions. BL 56 cm.

Spectacled Owl ▶

Like most owls, both sexes use calls to attract each other at mating time. Look for the nest-box in its cage. Most owls nest in tree holes in the wild. C. and S. America. BL 45 cm.

The female is slightly larger than the male

♀

♂

Tufts of feathers →

◀ Eurasian Eagle Owl

The feather-tufts are not ears; they help the birds recognize each other and may also express moods. Like all owls, its flight is quiet. Europe, Asia, N. Africa. Max. BL 71 cm.

◀ Caracara/ Carrion Hawk

Listen for its loud calls. In the wild, feeds mainly on carrion (dead meat). Notice its strong beak and claws, used for tearing meat. S. America. BL 55 cm.

Eagles

European Golden Eagle ▶

Like most birds of prey, the female is larger than the male. The courtship display is performed in the air. In the wild, catches prey with its clawed feet. Europe. BL 78 cm.

Its colour and size vary according to where it comes from and its age

Sharp claws

Hooked beak

◀ African Fish Eagle

Fed on meat and some fish in zoos. In the wild, dives to catch fish. Like most birds of prey, it has excellent sight. Noisy; throws its head back when calling.
Africa.
BL 74 cm.

♂

It has very long, pointed wings

Short tail

Bateleur Eagle ▶

When hunting in the wild, can glide for hours on its long wings. It has a spectacular courtship display in the air. Africa. BL 64 cms.

Condor, Vultures

Griffon Vulture ▶

Feeds on carrion (dead meat) in the wild. Vultures have bald heads (head feathers would get matted with blood when the bird was feeding). Usually lives in groups. Europe, S.W.Asia, S.Africa. Max. BL 1.1 m.

← *Comb*

The female Condor has red eyes and no comb or wattles

Wattles

♂

◀ Great Andean Condor

You may see it holding its wings extended; this allows the sun to warm them. Has a wing span of over 3 m. Female has red eyes and no lump on her beak. S.America. Max. BL 1.28 m.

American King Vulture ▶

During courtship in zoos, both sexes circle each other, whistling and flapping their wings. Unlike most birds, it probably uses its sense of smell to help it find food. C.and S. America. BL 80 cm.

The hook on the beak is used for tearing meat

Parrots

Scarlet Macaw
C.and S.America. BL 85 cm.
Blue-and-Yellow Macaw
S.America. BL 86 cm.
It has a strong beak which
can crack open hard fruits.
Notice its thick tongue.
Its feet are used for
holding food, and the
strong claws for gripping
branches. Most macaws
have long tails. They are
not good at mimicking
voices, but often scream
loudly or croak to each
other. Macaws and
cockatoos need strong
cages, as they can bite
through thick wire.

BLUE AND
YELLOW
MACAW

SCARLET ➚
MACAW

◄ African Grey Parrot
Very good at mimicking
voices. In the wild, lives in
large flocks. You may see
rings on the legs of caged
birds. These have numbers
on them to identify each
bird. W.and
C.Africa.
BL 33 cm.

◄ Sulphur-crested
Cockatoo
Screams when excited.
Male raises his crest when
courting, but both sexes
raise their crests at other
times.
Australia.
BL 50 cm.

Crest ➚

Parrots

Yellow-backed Lory ▶
Look for the nest box in
the cage. Most parrots
nest in tree-holes.
Molucca
Islands.
BL 30 cm.

All parrots
can use
their beaks
as hooks for
climbing

Fischer's Lovebird ▶
Pairs of lovebirds sit close
together; they groom
each other a lot. In the wild
they live in flocks.
E. Africa.
BL 15 cm.

◀ Rainbow Lorikeet
Its special tongue helps it
eat pollen and nectar; it
also eats fruit, leaves etc.
Very noisy.
Australasia.
BL 26 cm.

♂

◀ Cockatiel
Crest is held erect most of
the time. Makes a soft
chattering noise. It may
mimic.
Australia.
32 cm.

Crimson Rosella ▶
Eats mainly seeds,
spending a lot of time on
the ground. Chatters softly
while feeding.
S. and E. Australia.
BL 36 cm.

Toucans, Turaco, Minah, Hornbill

Ariel Toucan
Sulphur-breasted Toucan

The coloured bill may help birds of the same species recognize one another. In the wild, the large, but light bill and long, hard tongue help it pick fruit off trees. Needs room to leap from perch to perch to stop it getting fat. S. America. BL 52 cm.

SULPHUR-BREASTED TOUCAN

ARIEL TOUCAN

White-cheeked Turaco ▶

Has a dipping flight and strong feet for jumping and running along branches. It will raise its crest as a threat. W. Africa. BL 42 cm.

← Crest

This wing is stretched out to show the red flight feathers

Light-weight bill and horny casque

◀ Nepal Hill Minah

Can mimic voices well. At nesting time becomes aggressive; can be kept in groups at other times. S.E. Asia. BL 31 cm.

◀ Great Indian Hornbill

The large bill is light. At nesting time, the female walls herself into a hole leaving a slit through which the male feeds her. S.E. Asia. BL 1.2 m.

43

Roller, Pigeon, Motmot, Kookaburra

Lilac-breasted Roller ▶

Called roller because of its rolling, wheeling flight. Mates in flight. Hunts from a perch and takes food back to the same perch. Africa. BL 36 cm.

Blue-crowned Pigeon ▶

Largest pigeon in the world. Feeds on the ground, but will fly if alarmed. Nests and perches in trees. New Guinea. BL 68 cm.

The Motmot has a saw-edged bill

◀ Blue-crowned Motmot

Sits for long periods on its perch. Central parts of its tail feathers are bare from preening and being rubbed against objects. C. and S. America. BL 45 cm.

The top side of the tail is blue

◀ Kookaburra/ Laughing Jackass

Listen for its cackling call. In the wild, kills prey (reptiles and small mammals) by banging them against a branch. Australia. BL 46 cm.

Whydah, Starling, Hummingbird, Finches

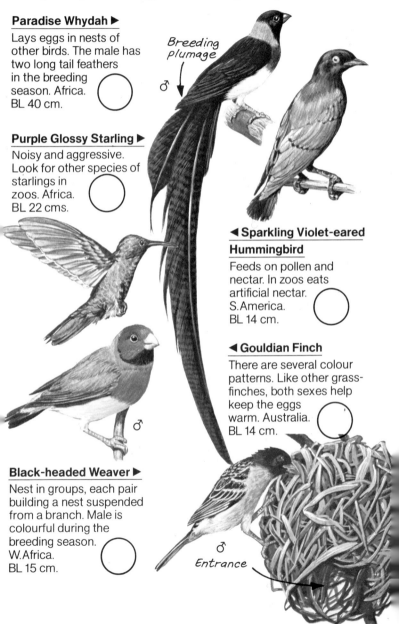

Paradise Whydah ▶

Lays eggs in nests of other birds. The male has two long tail feathers in the breeding season. Africa.
BL 40 cm.

Breeding plumage

♂

Purple Glossy Starling ▶

Noisy and aggressive. Look for other species of starlings in zoos. Africa.
BL 22 cms.

◀ Sparkling Violet-eared Hummingbird

Feeds on pollen and nectar. In zoos eats artificial nectar.
S.America.
BL 14 cm.

◀ Gouldian Finch

There are several colour patterns. Like other grass-finches, both sexes help keep the eggs warm. Australia.
BL 14 cm.

Black-headed Weaver ▶

Nest in groups, each pair building a nest suspended from a branch. Male is colourful during the breeding season.
W.Africa.
BL 15 cm.

♂

Entrance

Constricting snakes

Anaconda ▶

Non-poisonous. Spends a
lot of time in water. Like all
the snakes on this page,
it constricts (strangles)
its prey.
S. America.
Max. BL 11.5 m.

*Snakes
have no
outer ears*

◀ Boa Constrictor

Non-poisonous. Can climb
and has a slightly
prehensile tail. Mainly
nocturnal. Like all
constricting snakes, it is
fed several times a month,
depending on its size.
C. and S.
America.
Max. BL 5.5 m.

*All the
constricting
snakes can
open their mouths
very wide to
swallow large prey*

Indian Python ▶

S. E. Asia. Max. BL 7.6 m.
There are about 20
species of pythons. All are
non-poisonous. They lay
eggs (anacondas and
boas give birth to live
young). **African Python.**
Max. BL 5.5 m. **Reticulated
Python.** One of the world's
largest snakes. S. E. Asia.
Max. BL 10 m. **Royal/Ball
Python.** Curls into a ball if
frightened. W. Africa.
Max. BL 1.3 m. **Carpet
Python.** New Guinea,
Australia. Max. BL 4.3 m.

INDIAN PYTHON

AFRICAN PYTHON

ROYAL PYTHON

RETICULATED PYTHON

CARPET PYTHON

Snakes

Green Mamba ▶

Lives in branches. A fast mover. Like all snakes, it swallows its prey whole. Lays eggs.
Africa.
Max. BL 2.4 m.

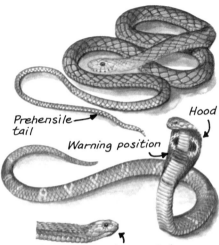

Hood

Prehensile tail

Warning position

Indian Cobra ▶

If frightened, its neck ribs move, expanding the skin to form a hood. It may then strike.
S. Asia.
Max. BL 1.8 m.

Head without hood expanded

Both vipers hiss when frightened

◀ Puff Adder

A viper. If frightened, puffs itself up to look threatening. All vipers give birth to live young.
Africa. BL 0.9 m.

◀ Gaboon Viper

Strikes from a coiled position. Long front fangs are folded back until it actually strikes.
Africa.
BL 1.2 m.

Eastern Diamondback Rattlesnake ▶

Shakes dry, loose scales on the end of its tail to give a warning rattle.
E. USA.
BL 1.5 m.

Rattle

Lizards

Common Iguana ▶

Has sharp claws and climbs well. Will lash out at an enemy with its long, powerful tail.
C. and S. America.
Max. BL 1.3 m.

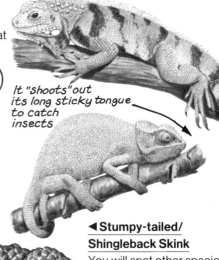

It "shoots" out its long sticky tongue to catch insects

Common Chameleon ▶

Skin changes colour or shade if it is excited, or if the light or temperature changes. Prehensile tail.
Mediterranean regions.
Max. BL 30 cm.

◀ Stumpy-tailed/
Shingleback Skink

You will spot other species of skinks in zoos.
Slow movers.
Australia.
Max. BL 45 cm.

◀ Leopard Gecko

Fast mover. Climbs well using special gripping pads on its feet.
S. Asia.
Max. BL 30 cm.

It lashes its tail when angry

Nile Monitor ▶

A good swimmer. Sharp claws for climbing, digging and defence. Tears its food with its sharp teeth.
Africa. BL 1.8 m.

Crocodile, Alligator, Turtle, Tortoise

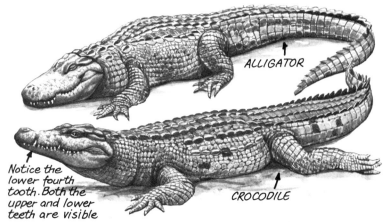

ALLIGATOR

Notice the
lower fourth
tooth. Both the
upper and lower
teeth are visible

CROCODILE

Mississippi Alligator

Like crocodiles, fed twice
a week on dead animals
or raw meat. Can replace
any lost teeth.
S.E. USA.
Max. BL 6 m.

Nile Crocodile

Stays very still most of the
time, but can move fast.
Can stay under water for
over an hour.
Africa.
Max. BL 5 m.

Carapace
(top shell)

Green Turtle

Vegetarian and has no
teeth. Leaves the sea to
lay eggs. Lives in warm
areas of Pacific, Atlantic
and Indian oceans.
Max. carapace
length 1.5 m.

Galapagos Giant Tortoise

Comes from the
Galapagos islands in the
Pacific ocean and is now
very rare. Lives to a great
age. Max.
carapace
length 1.5 m.

Nocturnal animals

Nocturnal means active at night. Usually the most active time for nocturnal animals is at dusk or when the moon is out, rather than at the darkest time of the night. Many of the larger animals also appear for short periods during the day if the sun is not too bright or if there is food available.

In zoos, most nocturnal animals sleep during opening hours, though some animals change their natural rhythms and are active in the day (for example the Leopard).

Some zoos have **nocturnal houses.** The lights in the houses are very bright at night; the animals think it is daytime and go to sleep. In daytime the lights are turned down so that they think it is dusk, or that the moon is shining, and come out to feed.

All nocturnals have at least one of their senses highly developed to help them cope with night life. Study each animal and see if you can work out which sense is most important.

Sight

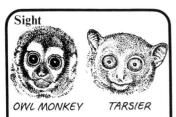

OWL MONKEY   TARSIER

Large eyes make it possible to see when there is very little light. In bright light, the animal narrows its pupils to protect the inner eye.

Hearing

JERBOA

BAT

Many nocturnals depend on hearing and have large ears. Bats have special hearing and can tell from echoes of their own noises where objects are.

Smell and Taste

FERRET BADGER   ANACONDA

Acute senses of smell and taste help animals find things in the dark. Snakes, usually semi-nocturnal, smell and taste with their tongues.

Touch

LEOPARD

SHREW

Some nocturnal animals use their noses or long whiskers to feel with. Snakes have no ears, but are very sensitive to ground vibrations.

Nocturnal animals

Slow Loris ▶

Moves carefully, always keeping two feet on the branch. Can climb upside-down and move on all fours on the ground. Sleeps curled in a ball.
S.Asia.
H&B 38 cm.

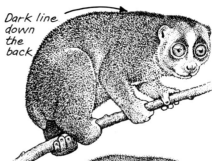

Dark line down the back

Slender Loris ▶

Has very mobile hip and ankle joints and you may see it in odd positions. Can catch flying insects with its hands.
Ceylon, S.India.
Max. H&B 25 cm.

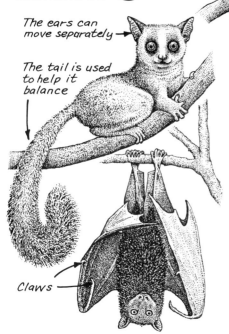

The ears can move separately →

The tail is used to help it balance

The Slender Loris can climb upside-down

Claws

◄ Senegal Bushbaby

Its fingers have pads to help it grip branches. Has strong back legs and can leap over 2 m. May use hands and feet to spread urine scent marks near its nest.
Africa. H&B 16 cm.

◄ Indian Fruit Bat

Unlike most bats, has no special echo-location sense. Has acute hearing and good sight; is helpless in total darkness. Noisy.
S.E.Asia.   Max. wingspan 1.7 m;
Max. H&B 40 cm.

51

Nocturnal animals

Common Opossum ▶

A marsupial with a pouch for its tiny young. Lives mostly on the ground, but uses its prehensile tail when climbing.
N. and S. America.
H&B 40 cm.

Prehensile tail used for climbing

Brush-tailed Possum ▶

A marsupial. Possums are from Australia, opossums from America. Climbs, using its prehensile tail as a fifth limb. Sleeps curled in a ball.
Australia.
H&B 55 cm.

Prehensile tail ⟶

Spines and fur

◀ Tasmanian Devil

A marsupial with a pouch for young. Runs with tail up and nose down, and is always snarling and sniffing. Powerful jaws and teeth. Rare in zoos. Tasmania.
H&B 60 cm.

◀ Echidna

A monotreme (lays eggs). Young are suckled in its pouch until their spines develop. Has very strong legs and digs very fast. No teeth and a tiny mouth at end of its snout. Feeds with a long sticky tongue. Australia.
H&B 60 cm.

Nocturnal animals

Hairy Armadillo ▶

An acute sense of smell, but poor eyesight. Spends a lot of time digging with its powerful front feet. Has a tough protective skin, but if frightened runs for its burrow. S.America. H&B 25 cm.

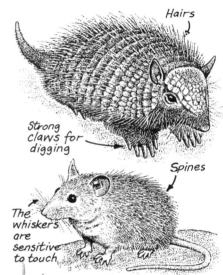

Hairs

Strong claws for digging

Spines

Spiny Mouse ▶

Has spines in the fur on its back. A fast mover, with good senses of sight and hearing and long whiskers, sensitive to touch. May also be active in the day. S.Asia, Africa. H&B 9 cm.

The whiskers are sensitive to touch

◀ Crested Porcupine

If frightened, will raise the long quills on its neck and back. It rattles them before attacking, and then sticks them into the enemy by backing into it. Will grow new quills to replace those lost. Africa. H&B 70 cm.

◀ Springhare/Springhaas

Related to rats and mice. In the wild, it digs burrows. Its sandy colouring helps conceal it in the sandy areas where it lives. S.and E.Africa. H&B 40 cm.

Attack position

Sandy colour

Sharp claws for digging

Nocturnal animals

Fennec Fox ▶

Acute sense of smell and huge outer ears, which in the wild may help it hear noises made by insects underground. Soles of feet are hairy.
Arabia, N.Africa.
H&B 40 cm.

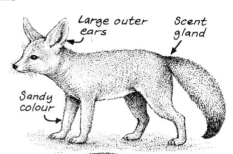

Large outer ears

Scent gland

Sandy colour

Raccoon ▶

Not wholly nocturnal. Very sensitive skin on paws; in the wild, uses its paws to catch animals in the water. In zoos, where it cannot fish, it replaces this activity by washing its food. N.and C.America.
H&B 60 cm.

◄ Striped Skunk

If frightened or angry, it will stamp its feet and raise its tail. This is the sign that it is about to squirt a foul-smelling liquid from its anal glands.
N.America.
H&B 30 cm.

Anal glands under the tail

◄ Kinkajou

Has a prehensile tail and in the wild lives in trees. In zoos, it is often on the ground. Very playful. Uses scent glands on the chin and belly to mark its territory. C.and S.America.
H&B 50 cm.

Prehensile tail

Nocturnal animals

Small Indian Mongoose ▶

Some mongooses attack and eat poisonous snakes. They are not immune to snake venom, but are fast and agile and usually escape being bitten. Ground living . S.E. Asia. H&B 30 cm.

Small-toothed Palm Civet ▶

A good climber and can leap between branches. Scent glands under the tail produce a musky smell used for marking the territory boundaries. S.E. Asia. H&B 50 cm.

◀ Binturong

Awkward on the ground, but a good climber. Tip of its tail is prehensile and can hold onto branches. Very noisy; spits and growls when angry. S.E. Asia. H&B 95 cm.

◀ Blotched Genet

Looks like a cat, but related to mongooses and civets. Fast moving and a good climber. Stalks its prey like a cat. Very inquisitive. S. and E. Africa. H&B 45 cm.

The tip of the tail is prehensile

55

Very rare animals

Unfortunately there are many rare animals in the world. Usually it is because they have been hunted for meat or for their skins, or because their habitat (the place where they live) is being destroyed. Extinction may occur naturally but is mainly caused by humans.

The best zoos are now trying to breed from their collections of rare animals so that new stocks of animals can be put back into the wild. A few animals, for example Przewalski's Horse, are only to be found in zoos and it is therefore very important that they should continue to breed in zoos.

The animals on these pages can only be spotted in a few zoos, but if breeding is successful, you may be able to see them in other zoos.

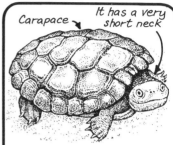

Carapace

It has a very short neck

Short-necked Tortoise
Not much is known about its habits. Found only near Perth, Australia, and is in Perth zoo.
Max. carapace length 14 cm.

Rabbit-eared Bandicoot
A marsupial or pouched animal. The opening of the pouch points towards the tail. It has silky blue-grey fur. Lives in Australia and is in Perth zoo (Australia).
Max. H&B 55 cm.

Giant Otter
Has a high-pitched, shrieking call. In six zoos, including Duisburg and Hamburg (Germany), and Madrid (Spain).
H&B 1.3. m.

Flat tail →

Kloss's/ Dwarf Gibbon

Its habits are like those of the other gibbons. Lives on islands off Sumatra. In three zoos, including Perth (Australia) and Basle (Switz). H&B 50 cm.

It stores fat at the base of its tail

Fat-tailed Dwarf Lemur

From Madagascar. In five zoos, including London (GB), Durham (USA) and Cologne (Germany). H&B 15 cm.

Tufts of fur on the ears

Spanish Lynx

Hunted for its beautiful spotted coat and is now nearly extinct in Spain. Can be seen in three zoos, including Barcelona (Spain) and Rome (Italy). H&B 1 m.

Fossa

A nocturnal carnivore from Madagascar. In four zoos, including Montpellier (France), Naples (Italy) and Basle (Switz.). H&B 70 cm.

Yellow fur on the ears and on the legs

Pale yellow rings on the tail

Yellow-footed Rock Wallaby

Found in rocky areas of Australia. In four zoos, including three Australian zoos: Perth, Penola and Adelaide. H&B 65 cm.

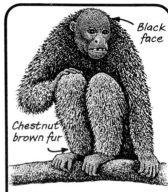

Black face

Chestnut brown fur

Black-headed Uakari

Lives in trees in tropical forests of S. America. In two zoos, including Cologne (Germany). H&B 55 cm.

Dark brown or black fur

Lowland Anoa

Lives in Indonesia and is in five zoos, including Antwerp (Belgium), Berlin (W. Germany), San Diego and Catskill (USA). SH 80 cm.

Caribbean Manatee

Lives off the coasts and in rivers in the Caribbean area. In six zoos, including Amsterdam (Holland), Miami Seaquarium, St. Augustine (USA). H&B 4.5 m.

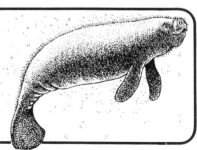

Britain

There are about 86 zoos in Britain. This is a list of some of the larger ones, with notes about any special features they have.

1 Jersey Zoo, Jersey. Rare species.
2 Padstow Bird Gardens, Cornwall.
3 Paignton Zoo, Devon. Big zoo. Gibbon island; reptile house.
4 Cricket St Thomas Wildlife Park, Chard, Somerset.
5 Bristol Zoo, Avon. Gorillas.
6 Slimbridge Refuge, Wildfowl Trust, Glos. Waterfowl.
7 Birdland Zoo Gardens, Bourton-on-the-water, nr Cheltenham, Glos.
8 The Falconry Centre, Newent, Glos. Birds of prey.
9 Lions of Longleat Park, Warminster, Wilts. White tigers; African animals; safari boat.
10 Marwell Zoological Park, Winchester, Hants. Rare hoofed animals. Carnivores.
11 Birdworld Zoo, Holt Pound, Farnham, Surrey.
12 Drusillas Zoo Park, Alfriston, Sussex.

13 Port Lympne, Zoo Park, Hythe, Kent.
14 Howletts Zoo Park, Bekesbourne, nr Canterbury, Kent. Breeding gorillas and tigers; rare species.
15 London Zoo. Big zoo. Nocturnal house; small mammals.
16 Chessington World of Adventure, Surrey. Big zoo.
17 Woburn Wild Animal Kingdom, Beds. Hoofed animals.
18 Whipsnade Zoo, Dunstable, Beds. Cheetahs.
19 Royal Windsor Safari Park, Windsor, Berks. Whale; dolphins; cheetahs; bears.
20 Cotswold Wildlife Park, Burford, Oxford. Reptiles.
21 Kilverstone Wildlife Park, Thetford, Norfolk. S. American animals.
22 Banham Zoo, Norwich, Norfolk.
23 Norfolk Wildlife Park and Pheasant Trust, Great Witchingham, Norfolk, European animals, pheasants.
24 Twycross Zoo, Atherstone, Warwicks. Proboscis monkeys; monkeys; apes.
25 Welsh Mountain Zoo, Colwyn Bay, Clwyd. American Bald Eagles.
26 Chester Zoo, Upton by Chester, Cheshire. Big zoo. Tropical house.
27 Blackpool Zoo, Lancs. Big zoo.
28 Glasgow Zoo, Glasgow.
29 Edinburgh Zoo. Big zoo.
30 Highland Wildlife Park, Kincraig, Inverness-shire.
31 Belfast Zoo, N. Ireland.

59

USA

This page lists only a selection of the 196 or so American zoos. Any special features of these zoos are mentioned after their addresses.

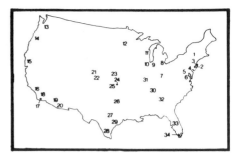

1 Catskill Game Farm, N.Y. Rare hoofed animals.

2 New York Zoological Park (Bronx Zoo), N.Y. Big zoo. Monkeys.

3 Staten Island Zoo, N.Y. Big zoo.

4 Philadelphia Zoo, Pa. Big zoo. Apes; reptile house; birds.

5 Catoctin Mountain Zoo, Thurmount, Md, Monkeys; apes; reptiles.

6 National Zoological Park, Smithsonian Institution, Washington D.C. Big zoo. Rare species; cats; Giant Pandas; reptiles; nocturnal house.

7 Cincinnati Zoo, Ohio. Big zoo.

8 Detroit Zoo, Mich. Big zoo. Polar Bears; penguins.

9 Chicago Zoo (Brookfied'Zoo), Ill. Big zoo. Dolphins.

10 Lincoln Park Zoo, Chicago, Ill. Big zoo. Apes; cats. S. American animals.

11 Milwaukee County Zoological Park, Wis. Big zoo.

12 Minnesota Zoo, Apple Valley, Minn. Habitat enclosures.

13 Woodland Park Zoo, Seattle, Wash. Nocturnal house.

14 Washington Park Zoo, Portland, Ore. Breeding elephants; cats.

15 San Francisco Zoo, Calif. Big zoo. Monkeys; apes; cats.

16 Los Angeles Zoo, Calif. Big zoo. Rare species; apes; cats.

17 San Diego Zoo, Calif. Big zoo. Rare species; Koalas; apes.

18 San Diego Wild Animal Park, Escondido, Calif. Hoofed animals.

19 Phoenix Zoo, Ariz. Big zoo. Arabian Oryx.

20 Arizona-Sonara Desert Museum, Tucson, Ariz. Desert animals.

21 Denver Zoo, Colo. Big zoo. Cats; waterfowl; monkeys.

22 Cheyenne Mountain Zoological Park, Colorado Springs, Colo. Monkeys; cats.

23 Topeka Zoo, Kan. Tropical rain-forest animals.

24 Tulsa Zoo, Okla.

25 Oklahoma City Zoo, Okla. Big zoo. Rare species; monkeys.

26 Fort Worth Zoo, Tex. Big zoo.

27 San Antonio Zoo, Tex. Big zoo. Antelopes; waterfowl.

28 Gladys Porter Zoo, Brownsville, Tex, Big Zoo. Rare species; duikers.

29 Houston Zoo, Tex. Big zoo.

30 Overton Park Zoo, Memphis, Tenn. Big zoo.

31 St Louis Zoo, Mo. Big zoo.

32 Atlanta Zoo, Ga. Big zoo. Reptiles.

33 Busch Gardens Zoo, Tampa, Fla. Big zoo. African animals; parrots.

34 Monkey Jungle, Miami, Fla. Semi-natural conditions.

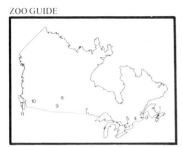

Canada

There are about 24 Canadian zoos. This page lists a few of them and mentions some of their special features.

1 Provincial Wildlife Park, Schubenacadie, N.S. Waterfowl.
2 Jardin Zoologique de Québec, Orsainville, Québec. Big zoo.
3 Société Zoologique de Granby, Québec. N. American animals.
4 Montréal Zoo, Québec. Big zoo.
5 Riverview Zoo Park, Peterborough, Ont. Pheasants.
6 Metro Toronto Zoo, Ont. Big zoo. Habitat houses; trails.
7 Assiniboine Park Zoo, Winnipeg, Manitoba. Big zoo. Rare species.
8 Alberta Game Farm, Edmonton, Albta. Rare hoofed animals.
9 Calgary Zoo and Natural History Park, St. George's Island, Albta. Big zoo. Northern animals; bears; cats.
10 Kamloops Wildlife Park, B.C. Canadian animals; reptiles.
11 Stanley Park Zoo, Vancouver, B.C. Canadian animals.

Australia

These are some of the 16 Australian zoos.

1 Perth Zoo, W.A. Big zoo. Australian animals; apes; birds.
2 Adelaide Zoo, S.A. Big zoo. Birds; wallabies.
3 Melbourne Zoo, Parkville, Vict. Big zoo. Australian animals; birds; walk-through houses.
4 Sir Colin Mackenzie Fauna Park, Healesville, Vict. Australian animals; Platypus.
5 Westbury Zoo, Tas. Tasmanian Devils.
6 Taronga Zoo, Sydney, N.S.W. Big zoo. Australian animals; Platypus; birds.
7 Australian Reptile Park, Gosford, N.S.W. Australian animals; reptiles.
8 Fleay's Fauna Reserve, West Burleigh, Queensland. Australian animals; Platypus.

New Zealand

These are three of the six New Zealand zoos.

1 Auckland Zoo. Big zoo. Nocturnal house; Kiwis.
2 Wellington Zoo. Chimpanzees.
3 Orana Park Wildlife Reserve, Christchurch. Drive-through zoo.

Europe

This is a list of some good zoos to visit if you go to Europe.

Austria
There are about six Austrian zoos.
Tiergarten Schönbrunn,
Vienna. Big zoo.

Belgium
There are about four Belgian zoos.
1 Antwerp Zoo. Big zoo.
2 Planckendael Zoo. Rare species.

Denmark
There are about six Danish zoos.
Zoologisk Have, Copenhagen. Big zoo.

France
There are about 36 French zoos.
1 Parc Zoologique de Paris.
2 Ménagerie du Jardin des Plantes, Paris. Big zoo.

West Germany
There are about 52 West German zoos.
1 Zoologischer Garten Berlin. Big zoo. Rare species; apes; birds.
2 Zoologischer Garten Köln, Cologne. Big zoo.
3 Zoo Duisberg. Big zoo. Dolphins; whales; Australian animals.
4 Zoologischer Garten Frankfurt/ Main. Big zoo. Reptile house; free-flight aviary; monkey house.
6 Carl Hagenbeck Tierpark, Hamburg. Big zoo.
7 Zoologischer Garten Hannover. Big zoo. Antelopes; elephants.
8 Krefelder Zoo, Krefeld. Big zoo. S. American animals; cats; apes.
9 Münchener Tierpark Hellabrunn, Munich. Big zoo. Apes; rare hoofed animals.
10 Wilhelma Zoologisch Garten, Stuttgart. Big zoo. Nocturnal house; apes.

Southern Ireland
Dublin Zoo. Cats.

Italy
There are about 21 Italian zoos.
1 Giardino Zoologico di Napoli. Big zoo. Antelopes; parrots.
2 Giardino Zoologico di Roma. Rome. Big zoo. Antelopes.

Netherlands
There are about 12 Dutch zoos.
1 Natura Artis Magistra, Amsterdam. Big zoo.
2 Rotterdamse Diergaarde. Big zoo. Birds of paradise; okapi; cats; monkeys; apes.
3 Dierenpark Wassenaar Zoo, Wassenaar. Big zoo. Birds.

Norway
Norway has three zoos.
Nordnesparken. Bergen.

Spain
There are about seven Spanish zoos.
1 Parque Zoologico de Barcelona. Big zoo. Spanish animals; white gorilla; dolphins.
2 Zoo de la Casa de Campo, Madrid.

Sweden
There are about ten Swedish zoos.
Boråsparken, Borås.

Switzerland
There are about ten Swiss zoos.
1 Zoologischer Garten Basel. Big zoo.
2 Zoologischer Garten Zürich. Big zoo. Vicunas.

Glossary

Browser – eats trees and bushes.
Canine teeth. - see page 5.
Carnivores - meat eaters. Also the name of an order of animals (see page 5) which includes bears, dogs, cats mongooses, weasels and their relatives. Most are meat eaters, but some also eat plant material.
Courtship/courting – behaviour during the breeding season when one sex shows off to the other sex to attract a breeding partner.
Dominant – a bossy animal. It may control other animals in its group. There may be a chain of dominance in groups. One animal will dominate one of the group, who in turn dominates another, and so on.
Genital area – the area around the sexual organs.
Herbivore – plant eater.
Inbreeding – when closely related animals (such as father and daughter) breed. Their young run the risk of being sickly or abnormal.
Omnivore - eats plants and meat.
Prehensile tail – a tail which can hold onto objects.
Scent glands – produce scent which is used mostly for marking territory or attracting a mate.
Species - see page 5.
Territory – some species of animals defend part of the area in which they live. This is their territory.
Territory marking – some animals use urine, dung or scent from scent glands to mark out points along the invisible boundary lines of their territory. This tells other animals of the same species where the territory starts and warns them not to enter. Calls and other signals may also be used.

Index